Light the Lamp

Poems Inspired by Sports

Charles Ames Fischer

Light The Lamp
Poems Inspired by Sports
by Charles Ames Fischer

Published by

SB
Sienna Books

ISBN: 978-1-940107-08-0 (Paper)

Book Design: Nick Zelinger, NZGraphics.com

First Edition

Published in the United States of America

In Memory of
My Father, Frederick Fischer

Introduction

Brimming with brilliant idioms, the sporting world is full of delightful language and wordplay. As a writer, I was always caught by expressions that made their way from the field or court to the couch or classroom, phrases like: *down to the wire, move the goalposts, win by a nose, out for the count, throw in the towel,* or *roll with the punches.* They have illuminating histories and contexts and become enlivened when woven into poetry. For example, "Light the Lamp" means to score a goal in ice hockey because a red light is turned on behind the net when the puck goes in. In a different context, it can mean to inspire or provide hope.

This book attempts to combine the wonders of poetry and the splendor of sports. Athletic enthusiasts can read this book to delight in discovering these idioms and, in some cases, even trying to determine which sport is suggested. Some of the poems are directly inspired, while others only make use of the sport's specific jargon. There are notes at the end of the book in case there is any doubt. Poetry fans can delight in the many turns of phrase from the sporting world that make for enjoyable reading. As an educator and writer, I hope to inspire everyone who reads this collection.

Author's Note

This book is in memory of my father, Frederick Fischer, who supported me in everything I did. Dad was a quiet man, and I never learned much about his life as a youngster. I knew he was a good athlete but was surprised when I came across his high school yearbook. He played four years of football, four years of basketball, two years of baseball, two years of track, and a year of volleyball.

His yearbook quote was, "Game is cheaper in the market than in the fields and woods." I have wondered about this saying many times and love how ambiguous it is. Does it mean, for example, that mass-produced food is literally less expensive? Could it possibly suggest that there is an additional mental or emotional cost to hunting? Certainly, hunting game involves more time and energy than simply picking up food at a market. Or could the word 'game' here suggest playing? Perhaps it means that indoor board games are cheapened life experiences compared to those out in the woods and fields. Or maybe, like a great saying, it means all of these and more. I wonder what it meant to him when he was in high school and whether the meaning changed at all over the course of his life.

I think Dad would have liked this collection of poems in his own way, and I hope you do, too.

Fred Fischer

*"The mind is not a cup to be filled,
but a lamp to be lit."*

Plutarch

(paraphrased)

Light the Lamp

First Period

"You miss a hundred percent of the shots you don't take."

Wayne Gretzky

Draft Prospect

Poetry is an immense
   world-river of wondrous words,
an ever surer creed of parading evidences
   and materialized magic,
      a cloud of eternal glory.

It is the divine illusion of destinies,
impassioned expression, the countenance
      of shadows and dreams, the
   breath of the finer spirit of knowledge:
thought and art in one accreditation.

Poetry obliterates distinctions between
   the finite and infinite, the
      conscious and unconscious,
sound and unsound or only half-sound,
   true and untrue or only half-true.

Everything which interferes with it,
      anything which hinders
   is injurious to the noble sphere
of the impassioned laws of
      poetical truth and lyrical beauty.

More and more humankind will discover
  that we have to turn to poetics
      to interpret life
to console us, to sustain us:
    sports are unconscious poetry.

Without it, our exploits are incomplete,
      sterile and arbitrary
full of dangerous dissatisfactions,
    placing a statue
        where there was once a person.

In Gretzky's Office

The Zamboni clears the page,
a fresh sheet of white.
I begin to write anew.
A puckish muse skates past,
releases frozen stanzas.

I collect the passes,
stick them on paper.
My short-handed goal is
to assist the process,
keep writing poetry.

The neutral zone trap
makes breakaways difficult.
A change on the fly often
facilitates development.

Finally, a wrist shot
from the blue line presents
a good scoring opportunity.
A little back-checking,
some cross-checking,
a few line changes.

Every poem requires scoring
a goal, notching an assist,
and getting into a fight
(or at least a rumble).

It's a Gordie Howe hat-trick
for this ardent poet.

The First Crossover

*Do the difficult things while they
are easy and do the great things
while they are small.*
                    ~Lao Tzu

Everything starts in the backcourt;
with enough drive we can fast break
away from recurring thoughts
and moving violations.

Box out, push everything
away from the paint,
prepare for an outlet pass.

Life is like that: emptying space,
filling space, banging the boards.
Empty the past, fill it with potential,
hope there's no lane violation.

Life's about rebounds, powering
forward, staying out of foul trouble,
avoiding the full-court press.

There are no free throws,
no easy scores, but we must
cross over half-court
before implementing a game plan.

We live at the top-of-the-key
where we can unlock the future,
escape the trap of zone defense.

The first crossover is the hardest;
others become easier with
time and practice.

Courtly Listening

is such a service for
another person,
a courteous gift of
heart and mind and soul.

Words carry no meaning until volleyed,
recognized, reflected, returned,
the follow-through vital.

A word without bounce is a deadball,
inertly dangerous; words with spin are
biased and unreliable.

The words we speak change,
transform when they come back to us,
vitamin-added
or
value-depreciated.

The goal of a good listener is to
remain in the mid-court,
neutral and full of curiosity.

It's imperative to listen through the racket,
to feel the vibration in the strings
of subtle communication.

Keep the cutline in mind, and if matters
corkscrew or counterdrop, it may
be necessary to kill contact.

Powerful listening involves stillness
and presence, deep inner calm,
the patience to make a prized return.

Whitewater Crafting

I wonder sometimes about my access;
it comes and goes in surges and swells,
often depending on the river rating.

The entrance angle is always important
to get a current line upstream and
follow the rapids to the end.

I find one of the keys is confluence,
where streams of thought combine
into a boil of whitewater words.

When I hit an eddying wall of doubt, I
send ahead a ghost boat of imagination,
hoping to make good time downriver.

I guide myself past the many gates,
maneuvering through each section,
cautious of reversals and undercuts.

Rounding bends, I await the technicals
that require critical skill and nuance,
the stern decision-making till take-out.

Steepness, roughness, volume, narrows
are all alluvial considerations
before the final manuscript is clean.

The last step is portage: publishing the book and bracing for the impact of all the crusty guides with lofty Pf.D's.

The Archer's Paradox

The instant you speak words,
you miss the mark.
          ~Zen proverb

When you reach the back wall
and your options appear to narrow
the easy solution is to nock an arrow,
let fly a brace of quivering words,
(perhaps an unkind bolt or two).

When your words miss the mark,
understand you can always apologize,
recurve the whole situation; know
oftentimes it's the archer—
                    sometimes the bow.

Even when your words hit the target,
understand the need for flexibility
since you might have missed the moral;
oftentimes it's the archer—
                    sometimes the quarrel.

When you reach the back wall
and your options appear to narrow
the easy solution is to nock an arrow,
but a better choice is Sun Tzu's counsel:
the greatest victory involves no battle.

Six Degrees

The election was rigged!
The playoffs were rigged!
Those trials were rigged!
What the truth is, I don't know,
but at least my sailboat
is rigged and ready to go.

Weigh anchor... I'm underway
because what's to be gained in
the safety of being stationary?
Leaving the harbor will be hard,
I know, but at least my sailboat
is rigged and ready to go.

I'm not worried about failing
because I'm sailing, and
there's never a straight course.
Heave all the insults you want;
I will not yaw. Try to sway me
with wiles; I will not pitch.
Lure me to surge or slow;
I'll never roll, for my sailboat
is rigged and ready to go.

I know the ropes;
I am seeking six degrees of separation
from the flotsam and jetsam
of a listless life. I'm tired of
the scuttlebutt and chin-wagging,
the political spindrift prose. My
life is too precious for undertow;
good thing my sailboat
is rigged and ready to go.

Receiving the Future

Mastering others is strength.
Mastering yourself is true power.
~Lao Tzu

Broken plays are often
the most creative:
pass attempts, rush attempts.
There's a regularity we must shed,
otherwise there are far too many
automatic first downs.

Shattered patterns, fumbles,
past interference;
all might delay our game,
but it's about forward motion,
field position, total yardage.

We're all working toward
the end zone in whatever
increments we can manage.

Occasionally, though, even
a no-huddle offense isn't quick
enough. Sometimes, the best
thing to do is break formation
and ensure that we are
an eligible receiver.

Cadences of Living

Alter your stride and
meet a stranger—you.
~Anonymous

You don't know who you are
until you've run long and hard
enough to change the landscape,
the song in your heart pushing tempo:
it's you, verses, the trail.

You might hit a wall early or set a course record,
run hot, run cold in intervals,
find better running economy,
but do you run happy?

You've sprinted, you've surged
in and out of the training zone,
but have you checked and challenged
the content of your character?

Keep changing,
knowing the work is always ongoing,
the song in your heart pushing,
pushing tempo:
run hard or walk home.

It's training to run,
not running to train:
exercise and exorcise are
a varsity letter apart.

Yearn to feel the burn? Yes, yes,
your recovery is on
the other side of the threshold.

All-Star Cheers

Hey people! Hey people!
Hey people of Earth!
It's time to rewind
and show us your worth.

Hey, you Green Emerald fans,
stand up and clap your hands!
Go Emeralds! Go Knights!
Go Emeralds! Go Knights!

We're hoping you
will stunt to
new heights,
new heights.

We are the Spotters,
the mighty, mighty Spotters!
And we're hoping you
will break through—
break through the banner.

Hey, you paper doll people,
it's time to show and go.
Show us your spirit,
clap your hands,
stomp your feet!
Show us your spirit,
level seven elite!

Hey, you Green Emerald fans,
get up and wave your hands!
Go Emeralds! Go Knights!
Go Emeralds! Go Knights!

Props to you
if you double-stunt
to new heights,
new heights!

We're hoping you
will fly to—
fly to our lights!

We are the All-Stars,
the mighty, mighty All-Stars!
And we're hoping you
will break through—
break through the banner!

Balance and Movement

When you reach the top of the mountain
there's only downhill to go,
though a bit of backcountry
can lead to a higher peak.

Some alpine touring or a special lift
can help you reach the next summit.
It's necessary to go down
before going up
before going down again.

This is the nature of life:
down and up only appear to be opposites.
In reality, there is just balance and movement,
and even those blur in swirling snow.
You must often slalom down before
being able to go straight to the top.

Being at cross-purposes will cause
your lines to chatter, loosen base layers,
and delay your freestyle journey.
It's necessary to stop
before going
before stopping again.

This is the nature of life:
stop and go only appear to be opposites.
In reality, there is just balance and movement,
and even those blur with impermanence.

It's at the bottom of the run where you
will lodge your developments,
keep your bindings, and reboot
your personal enterprise.

The Law of Alternation

The game is Ping-Pong,
as if warning of the double-bounce.
Ping a serve. *Pong* a return.
But Ping-Pong on one side
and the point is lost.

Ping-Pong has that magical sing-song
sweet spot sound so soft to hear.
Pong-Ping doesn't have the same ring—
wrong backspin on the ear.

When speaking pings, listening pongs.
When others agree, we feel strong.
When words sting, we feel wronged.

As Ace of the solar system, the
yellow sun rings blue earth songs;
when sunlight pings a leaf, green pongs.

It's the alternation of law: spins
and counter-spins, the endless helix
that underpins the universe.

In the Home Stretch

I wouldn't know how to act
except for emulating those around me
counterfeiting copies,
reproduction ongoing.
So I am a person
on the starting line,
a paper-chain person,
neck and neck,
not yet myself,
never quite someone else.

I wouldn't know how to think
except for imitating those nearby
repeating words,
language compounding.
But I am an individual
across the board,
hitting my stride
in the morning line,
not yet thinking much,
almost there, under the wire.

I wouldn't know how to write
except for the marvels of poetry
hands down,
lines glistening.
I am a poet
finally on the inside track,
thoroughbred lines
down each page,
not one the same, no
never one the same.

Second Period

*"To give any less than your best
is to sacrifice a gift."*

Steve Prefontaine

Field Position·

We live in a wicket system
where average isn't enough to
fill all the bend-the-back quotients.
Someone has to farm the strike
but somehow we all fall
short of length in the
corridor of uncertainty.

When deliveries arrive,
full-pitched or short-pitched,
go short or go deep,
go square or go long,
go wide or go fine,
go silly if you must;
it's the approach that counts.

Everyone wants a featherbed, but
life's full of stumps and bails.
Doubt is the death rattle that
will lead to a batting collapse.
At times we're caught out,
sometimes bowled over,
many times stumped.

We live for the fall of wicket,
when we can cross the rope
into broad freedom. We can
be ourselves off the field,
carry the bat whenever
and wherever we want.

Karma

A cartwheeling code of points
start value adjusted for difficulty
based on back-to-back tumbling

learn what you can from the vault
raise your efforts on uneven bars
improve your current floor routines

do not get stuck dwelling on rings
work on your release move and
plan for a dynamic dismount.

On the Level Pitch

If Light is in your heart, you
will find your way home.
~Rumi

You are the keeper of your destiny;
   on the pitch ahead of you
your inner lives provide full support,
   center strength and striker capabilities.
Depending on your formation,
   you may or may not have wings.

If you play the game well, you will
   earn added time, especially when
you learn to bend around walls.
   Counter-press when you can;
take your punches early so
   you can corner kick later.
How many different caps will you
   earn in the course of your life?

The goal is to win a world cup,
   the golden grail of achievement:
living a life of purity & steadfastness,
   despite playing in front of empty arenas.
Before you hang up your boots, ask:
   Was I offside too many times?
Was I red-carded once too often?
   Did I collect enough silverware?

Put Some Points on the Board

To be tactical with your life
be syntactical—may your words,
no matter how varied or arranged,
carry the content of your integrity;
wear an indelible uniform of honor.

The reason is simple: every
string of words spoken aloud is
a reflection of your character,
Walk your talk measured
in miles of merriment
or millimeters of complaint.

Play to your strengths and
Give it your best shot
do not begin to express the overlays
of importance, because we know
*Offense sells tickets, but
defense wins championships.*

Every word contains force,
and forces aggregated
author your future: *Start the
way you mean to finish.*
How you call the shots
on the field will decide how
you'll be arranged underneath.

The Great Aim

The cave you fear to enter
may hold the light you seek.
                    ~Rumi

The Great Aim is to change.
What could be better than changing?
Certainly not staying the same.
Who would want to be forever riding
without upgrade and growth?

Consider the alchemy of sleep. Imagine
waking up after a day of hot friction,
boneless and delaminated,
never able to recover.
Sleep is a cleansing gift, a blunt
reminder that change is good.

Kickflip: What's on deck for your life?

The trick is versatility. Grind goofy-footed
and unleash new balances. Ride and glide,
flip and spin. Airwalk, ollie, land a 900,
grab melancholy and darkslide into light.

Try everything and then land the impossible.
Get a grip on speed wobble and keep
your bearings. Do something extraordinary.
You have a destiny. Why not carve it?

Drag Suit

It's a drag wearing bones and skin,
carrying the weight of water,
flat-starting here on Earth, collecting
gravitas, emitting gravity waves.

This drag suit is for training purposes.

The short course is harder to find
and more difficult to race against
the tide of the clock, the flip turns
more numerous but essential.

Long course rebirth is easier to grasp,
simpler to stay in a lane where we can
lap loneliness and freestyle ourselves
from the spinning arms of the collective.

We are spiritual beings experiencing
a heavy existence. Collecting light
in the catch phase is the key to
achieving escape velocity.

When it's time to touch out
and exit these iridescent waters,
we'll need to provide proof of time
before entering the next ready room.

Personal Best

The ultimate contest, track & field
where I will not break, I will not yield
faster, farther, higher, stronger
I'll challenge myself for personal best
track & field, the ultimate contest.

Athletic height of competition, field & track
sprints and hurdles, relays, distance laps
stronger, faster, farther, higher
I ready myself in power position
field & track, athletic height of competition.

The ultimate contest, track & field
for vaults and jumps I get myself steeled
higher, stronger, faster, farther
I will not cut curves, I will not rest
track & field, the ultimate contest.

Athletic height of competition, field & track
discus, shot, javelin— I'll get the knack
farther, higher, stronger, faster
My dreams will come to fruition
field & track, athletic height of competition.

The ultimate contest, track & field
where intense training is my shield
faster, farther, higher, stronger
I'll challenge myself for personal best
track & field, the ultimate contest.

Dancing with the Stars

I love skating on the orbital plane,
     synergizing with planets in their flying spins,
         pattern-dancing around the solar system.

I mirror-skate with Mercury's layback spin
     and join Jupiter's giant axel-jump,
         Saturn's lasso lift of moons and icy rings.

I twizzle and turn with Neptune,
     glide cantilever with Uranus,
         free dance with Mars,
and split jump alongside Venus.

I enjoy a short program in the asteroid field
     and bracket turn a time or two with Earth,
         edge jump out past Pluto.

I like to finish with my signature move,
     an I-spin picked up from the sun, but
         swizzled with my own combination.

Assembling the Perfect Fantasy Football Team

The dream begins early in the summer
before the leaves begin to whorl
and the hints of September waver on the wind.

Process each portentous piece of information,
slowly savor the in-depth details—
whether regarding a running back or kicker,
contemplating a QB or a wide receiver.

Dynasty – We'll save you 20% or more on injury insurance

Search for the staggering statistic,
the one that can puncture any game—
it's the beau ideal we strive for every season.

Blessed with fanatical foresight and a little luck,
get at least one big-time receiver early.
Later, think: player first, position second.

Dynasty – We'll save you 20% or more on injury insurance

Fantasy leagues are won with superstars;
don't give in to the gravity of groupthink.
Trust your own player evaluation;
even the experts have blind spots.

It's better to draft a fantastic player
you believe in a round too early
than a single pick too late.

Dynasty – We'll save you 20% or more on injury insurance

For My Coaches, Who Stressed Defense

On the slow ice,
in early mornings under the dim lights, we practiced
the long discipline of defense. I watched from
the blue line,
the red line, the bench,
as they carved the ice, bodies
and sticks positioned for back-checking.
They could block every pass
through the lanes. I admired their technique, but
not enough
to tear my eyes away from the scoreboard
that loomed over the arena.

Seasons passed, long periods of minor league play,
countless lines. I could snipe from any angle,
find the back of the net with ease, and yet
they stressed the same fundamentals:
the stick positioning and hustle, the
precise pressure. That unwavering emphasis
on the basics of defense,
and I never learned what they were winging.

Like a slow whistle in the D-zone,
let this be the signal
I'm finally grasping the importance of discipline.

Quick Peaks

It's too easy to see mountain
climbing as a metaphor for life;
the top of the mountain being
the tip of the iceberg and all that.

The problem is when you reach top
you can only go down from there, like
people who peak too early in high school
and slowly descend into darker days.

But since playing around with metaphors
puts a simile on my face, here we go.

> Too many people are peak-baggers,
> trail-cutters, so intent on alpine style
> that they completely miss the deadpoint.
> It's not the destination, it's the journey;
> too much back-clipping, headwalling,
> hand-jamming; there's only so many
> crimps, crampons, and crash pads you
> can use to get out of the isolation zone.

> I once feared the Bermuda Triangle, spent
> sleepless nights worried about quicksand.
> Now I know it's the American Death Triangle
> I should have feared most: the fashionista
> accessories, the distracting summits,
> the immaterial made material.

A-Line to the Stars

To the mind that is still, the
whole universe surrenders.
~Lao Tzu

Step up, step down,
put your armor on,
get into attack position;
it's time to ride lightning,
thunder through chunder
and shift with purpose.

Step down, step up,
enter the flow trail,
stoked and starry-eyed;
it's hero dirt you're after,
fast moving faster.

To be a qualifier
you must shred ahead,
shed behind, travel the trail
with body and mind,
sailor soul in full control.

The ride down is difficult
and up is impossible, but
do it anyway; the peak
is just a physical limit
to overcome.

Look up, look up,
take your armor off,
get into aligned position;
it's time to ride, lightening
yourself for the Milky Way.

Roundtripper

People don't take trips—
trips take people.
~John Steinbeck

It's vital to stay ahead of the count;
there is safety in perseverance
so ignore the brushback pitches,
the high heaters buzzing your tower.

Stay focused on clearing the bases.
Find your swing, and when the time
comes, don't miss that perfect pitch.

Never strike out looking. Work
the count, find your flow, and
when that curve finally comes,
put a charge on the ball.

Keep yourself honest: it's not
the bat that hits the ball; it's
the power of the mind—the bat is
merely an extension of intention.

The goal is to go deep, go yard,
or grab some pine and go home.
The game is decided by inches
so put on a rally cap,
prepare for a moonshot.

Never forget to touch all bases.
Don't be a one-game wonder;
you want to return after
crossing the plate.

Service

The first serve is paying back
    for the life that was given to you
by the entry system. Weren't you
    blessed with a beautiful body?
Weren't you invited to qualifiers?

The second serve is a slice of life;
    there's no room for unforced errors.
Whatever happens, do not double-fault
    on the loan of your soul and spirit, the
chip-and-charge of your body & mind.

Expect a return on investment,
    otherwise there'll be an upset.
In any ensuing rally, watch the
    backswing; plan for a passing
shot down the alley.

Hopefully, your first tour on Earth
    will be a break point and provide
an advantage out; otherwise you
    may find yourself a flatliner
and lose match point.

Living is about creating topspin
    action at a distance, ensuring
your future with the final line judge.
    Return interest; otherwise, you'll
be ghosting a dead net.

Third Period

*"If you don't have time to do it right,
when will you have time to do it over?"*

John Wooden

Permanent Line

Bottom-bouncing? Floundering?
    Feeling barbless?
The key is often deep-dropping,
    returning to the source of
your inspiration, your emergence.
    The goal is to become
a monofilament, a permanent line,
serendipity spinning forward,
    never blind-casting
    never back-lashing.

It helps to feather that line;
    a bit of angling can change
even the spiniest outlook.
Spincast your passion, wind in
    all the slack lines
until you are free reeling.
After that, it's about patience,
    jigging carefully enough
to land the strongest standard:
    the most powerful principle
    you can catch and keep.

Grand Spiral Technical Briefing

Home is not where you are born;
home is where all your attempts
to escape cease.
          ~Naguib Mahfouz

We race laps around the sun,
      birthdays coming and going,
seeking speed and airtime,
      shredding over corrugations,
finessing out of crossruts,

but it's easy to forget that
      the entire track travels
through the universe,
      the final finish line never
where you first suspect.

The question arises: Are
      you living your freestyle life
or are you just a tourist?

There's always a double track:
      the circular short-shift and
the long-view immortal line.
      To avoid an involuntary
dismount, stay in the
      zone of importance,
remember to regrip and rip.

The Curve of Perception

I remember those Wiffle Ball days
    of navigating middle school;
there was always such a variety
    of pitches to worry about:
fastballs, sinkers, sliders, change-ups.

We wanted to know so many things:
    how to ask girls to dance,
how couples got together, how
    to stay ahead in the count,
how a ball could bend so much.

We learned that things break differently
    depending on speed and spin, how
much of a grip we had social cues.
    The big lesson we had to absorb
was that the biggest curveballs
    were never pitches.

When we wanted to find out if a girl liked
    us back, we'd ask her friends and,
inevitably, be left standing there by
    our lockers, confused, wondering how
even simple words like
    YES or NO could curve so much.

Behind in the Count

Mom played pro softball and my older
sister's playing D-1. I'm at tryouts, everyone
wondering if I can finally make varsity,
close the book in my final batting practice.

I step to the batter's box, ready to put a
charge on the ball. The pitcher windmills,
throws a rising heater over the heart
of the plate that freezes me.

                          But my shadow
reaches out, slaps a single to short right field.
A crow-hop curve, and my silhouette bat
hits an opposite field blooper. Every pitch
keeps me honest, and only my shadow
seems to have any plate discipline.

                          "Sorry, kid,"
coach says. "Didn't your family tell you never
to strike out looking at tryouts?"

                               Yeah,
I want to say, but I'm caught leaving early
and my shadow stays behind in the box.
I pick up a foul ball in the grass and roll
it down the line to the catcher.

Wrestling Truths

There are two types of understanding
we can attempt to pin:
minor truths and Major Truths.

Minor truths move and morph, fluctuating on the time,
the current circumstances, the relative position. Cradle
a minor truth and a quick reversal can change levels,
shift the match. Minor truths are freestyle, appear
outside, only to take an inside position in your mind.

Major TRuths are unchanging and fixed, no matter what
appears to dictate the action. They are the bridges to the
natural laws of the universe. Circle around Major
TRUths and you will discover no easy way to initiate an
effective grapple, though nature holds many clues.

Offense and defense, left and right, home and away,
night and day, Major TRUThs first appear on the mat as
opposites. Outside the ring, we can see the numbers:
     three is a key: positive, neutral, negative;
     four is a door: winter, spring, summer, autumn;
     five comes alive, six becomes fixed, seven is leaven,
     eight is a gate, and nine is the shrine.

There's a total effort with Major TRUTHs; we cannot simply play the edges, passively awaiting a first move. Major TRUTHS are elusive, but we can count on creating angles, completely activating our inner lives, holding fast and thinking slow, and never, never letting go.

Dialogue, in Volleys

First, the serve: off-speed politeness,
floating ideas, overhand optimism,
getting into ready position,
uncertainty and apprehension,
roles and responsibilities,
goals and expectations.

Then, the bump from the baseline
into the storm of attack lines, passing
leadership, giving and receiving feedback,
the crucial need for effective listening.
Power struggles interrupt flow;
oscillations and errors preside.

Third: processes and procedures,
comfortable and confident finesse,
the freedom to contribute to the team.
Assisting the development of trust,
passing for the perfect set:
mastership and teamwork.

Last, the spike of clarity, the backcourt
collaboration scoring an important point,
avoiding the five common errors:

letting an idea get blocked,
getting stuck in the net of confusion,
crossing over an ethical centerline,
making unauthorized connections,
guiding an idea out of bounds.

Afterwards, the eventual slow-down,
adjourning and tying up loose ends,
some rewards, restlessness, and relief,
and hopefully, no lasting signs of grief.

Approaching the Fairway

It's not how good your shots are;
it's how good your bad shots are.
~Anonymous

We can always seek multiple directions
From the tee, where dreams take flight;
Do not chase hole-in-one perfection.

We can improve drive with iron selection,
From the fairway, where we gather light;
We can always seek multiple directions.

We can create links and make connections
From the rough, learn wrong from right,
But do not chase hole-in-one perfection.

We can refine ourselves with introspection
From the hazards, where we learned to fight;
Still, we can always seek multiple directions.

We can revise our goals with course corrections
Out of traps, where we struggle to stay bright,
But do not chase hole-in-one perfection.

We can find breaks with gradient inspection,
Upon the green, where we set our sights.
We can always seek multiple directions,
But do not chase hole-in-one perfection.

How to Change Your Mind

Look for new alleys
Be open to different delivery styles
Change your angle of entry
Ignore the seven regular arrows
Turn splits into advantages
Recognize conditioner patterns
Alter your approach to fit different lanes

An inquisitive mind can always adapt
Stay anchored in awe and wonder
Ask questions and follow through
Keep score of your best ideas
A winning end is a strike away

Frame and re-frame the problem
Count every point carefully
Examine all the options
Never underestimate a rogue pin
Consider handicaps and consequences

Anticipate any breakpoints
Challenge spare assumptions
Calculate future traction:
Skid distance, hook rotation, roll-out

Expect drift and burn out
Disrupt delivery routines
Don't expect a perfect game
Roll for high average.

Into Space

Our bodies are lumps of gravity:
head, shoulders, torso, hips
moving through synchrony,
footwork, armwork, alignment,
all in formulation for
balance into movement,

movement into action,
slows and quicks, extensions,
amalgamations, turns and sways;
the moving center sweeps us
along curves of progression.

Then the promenade into space:
posture, poise, and frame,
the instinctive floor craft
guiding the dancer into the

swing of time: rise and fall, the
upper motion of the metronome,
the lower pivot of the pendulum

into the energy of the system: flow
and force, tension and weight,
the electricity between partners,
all in the formulation of
balance into movement, back
into balance once again.

We move to occupy new space, like
all living things trying to discover
new possibilities, gliding and circling,
turning and spinning like galaxies.

The Gain Line

If you have the guts to keep making
mistakes, your wisdom and intelligence
leap forward with huge momentum.
       ~Holly Near

Too often we go to our set pieces,
trying to gain advantage
yet even a quick ankle tap
can easily bring us down.

It's an incongruity, really;
what makes us think what
worked in the past will
work in the future? It's
one thing to plan ahead,
another to stay locked in phase,
tunnel-vision preventing
any efforts to adapt.

Being in the ruck and scrum
of life is a slow and tiresome
line ahead, the group of death
plodding that does not
propel us forward at pace.

Line break, line out,
it's up and under and around
that will win the day,
spreading wings that will
speed us to our goals.

The key is to develop a try line;
those old plays are just
blood substitutions, one
short plank for another.

Goals, in Life

At 100 yards, I feel cut off,
drifting along the end line,
wasting time in long corners.

At 50 yards, over-gripped
with intention; hands sweaty,
I prepare to switch fields.

At 25 yards, I'm channeled in,
seeking advantage, ready to
split the defense.

At 16 yards, I'm in the zone;
this is my time, for me,
so very much for me.

At 8 yards, I question my goals.
What's the best position for me?
Where do I fit on this team?

At 4 yards, I realize I belong to
so many teams in life, and there's
no 'I' in team, as they say.

At 2 yards out, worlds collide.

Inward now, under the surface,
I can be myself here in the flow
where time and soul are one.

Inward still, the breakaway—
me and we interchangeable.

Changing Planes

If you pick up one end of the stick,
you also pick up the other.
                    ~African proverb

My mother always encouraged me
to stick things out, never quit.
Which meant once I started something
I had to see it through to the end.
I learned the hard way that
there are two types of aims:
short-stick and long-stick.

Short-stick aims are achieved
through intensity and speed,
changing planes, creating angles,
coordinating attacks.

Long-stick aims are achieved
through patience and persistence,
reducing angles, defending space,
breaking opportunities.

I became a goaltender, more
interested in making saves and
helping others achieve
their aims. I learned to quickly
leave the crease, pass on
my opportunities as a teacher.

Small aims can be abandoned,
ball down, simply walk away.
Many are fleetingly important
and can be cradled in case a
give-and-go increases a
scoring opportunity. I have
found that a good stick-check
appraisal can determine longevity.

An important aim requires you to
keep it in the box for the duration,
flag down, do everything you can
to maintain possession. Sometimes
you have to square-up and deal
with any unfortunate consequences.
Learn to roll dodge and stick a game
plan that remains fluid and exciting.

Playing sports, never quitting, has taught
me a vital lesson: sometimes you have
to change coordinate planes to keep
unimportant things unimportant
and important things important.
Short-stick goals start high, end low;
Long-stick goals start low, end high.

Those Hockey Weekends
(Thank You, Dad)

Oh, those weekends when my father
    got up even earlier, roused my skeleton
in the frosty darkness. He'd scrape the
    windshield, warm the car before
I'd even assembled myself downstairs.
    I don't recall ever thanking him.

He drove me to all the early practices,
    the snow-distant away games. He never
said much, mostly smoked his corncob pipe,
    gave me a few pointers on my form.

Sometimes we stopped at a diner
    where he always ordered black coffee,
hash, and bacon—extra crispy. He'd share
    the same jokes, tell the same stories.
What did I know then of love?
    What do I know of it now except poetry?

Overtime

"Watch your thoughts, for they become words.
Watch your words, for they become actions.
Watch your actions, for they become habits.
Watch your habits, for they become character.
Watch your character, for it becomes your destiny."

Anonymous

Notes on Select Poems

"Draft Prospect"
Mostly a found poem from Matthew Arnold's essay "The Study of Poetry" (1880).

"In Gretzky's Office"
Inspired by my favorite sport: ice hockey.

"The First Crossover"
Thinking about basketball and the timeline of life.

"Courtly Listening"
Inspired by squash and racquetball.

"Whitewater Crafting"
Pf.D.'s is a joke about Ph.D.'s. In the rafting world, it stands for Personal Floatation Device (life jacket).

"Receiving the Future"
Inspired by American football.

"Cadences of Living"
Inspired by running, cross-country or otherwise.

"All-Star Cheers"
Could the stars possibly be our cheerleaders?

"Balance and Movement"
Inspired by skiing, cross-country and downhill.

"In the Home Stretch"
A little horseracing, a little writing.

"Field Position"
Inspired by cricket.

"Karma"
Inspired by gymnastics.

"On the Level Pitch"
Inspired by soccer (football).

"The Great Aim"
Inspired by the risk-taking so inherent in skateboarding.

"Drag Suit"
Inspired by the thought of swimming through the universe.

"Assembling the Perfect Fantasy Football Team"
In part, a found poem from *Sports Illustrated* 2015 Fantasy Football guide, complete with an advertisement.

"For My Coaches, Who Stressed Defense"
An homage to David Bottoms, a pastiche modeled
after his poem: "Sign for My Father, Who Stressed
the Bunt."

"A-Line to the Stars"
Inspired by mountain biking, and the idea of riding
forever upward.

"Roundtripper"
Inspired by baseball.

"Service"
Inspired by tennis.

"Permanent Line"
Inspired by the thought of fishing for important
values and principles.

"Grand Spiral Technical Briefing"
Inspired by motocross and similar sports.

"Dialogue, in Volleys"
Inspired by how conversations can feel like playing
volleyball.

"How to Change Your Mind"
Inspired by bowling.

"Into Space"
Inspired by ballroom dancing and the movement of the spheres.

"The Gain Line"
Inspired by rugby.

"Goals, in Life"
Loosely inspired by field hockey, but a lot to do with how close or far away things in life can feel from a goalie's perspective.

"Changing Planes"
Inspired by lacrosse and changing angles.

"Those Hockey Weekends (Thank You, Dad)"
An homage to Robert Hayden, a pastiche modeled after his poem titled: "Those Winter Sundays."

Acknowledgments

My thanks to the following people, somewhat in chronological order. I don't remember reading or writing much poetry until college. Of course, I had come across Dr. Seuss and Shel Silverstein as a youngster, but I hadn't really been exposed to many poets. So, thank you to my college professor and poetry mentor, Ruth Stone, for being so patient with me. Even so, I wrote mostly fiction in college and didn't write a lot of poetry until I started teaching elementary school. So, thank you to my colleague, Kevin Brodeur, for introducing me to a poetry anthology project, which evolved into my favorite unit to teach. And special thank-yous to the many writing companions over the years who pushed me to do weekly assignments and spontaneous on-demand writings and for encouraging my study of words and language at much deeper levels. You know who you are.

Thank you also to my students at St. Anne's-Belfield School for inspiring me to connect sports and poetry. Thank you to Brian Gulotta for reading and giving me feedback on an early draft. And to Alison Gulotta for editing and making amazing suggestions. Thank you to Nick Zelinger, Judith Briles, and Author U for helping to bring my projects to life.

Also by
Charles Ames Fischer

Creative Thinking Cards

Creative Thinking Cards is the first deck in a series and contains 50 cards for all manner of creative enterprises. As the flagship set, they come with a 42-page explanatory booklet full of useful prompts and ideas. These cards will change the way you see everything!

- Learn new strategies for creative thinking.
- Explore hundreds of ideas and combinations.
- Prompt creativity in powerful, collaborative ways.

Creative Thinking Cards: Zany Supplemental

The *Creative Thinking Cards: Zany Supplemental* is a 52-card additional resource for all creative endeavors. Designed by a teacher with classroom activities in mind, these cards will enhance the way you see everything and push your creativity to new levels!

- Enjoy even more abstract images.
- Explore quixotic quotations.
- Integrate oblique emojis.
- Ponder wonderfully inventive words.

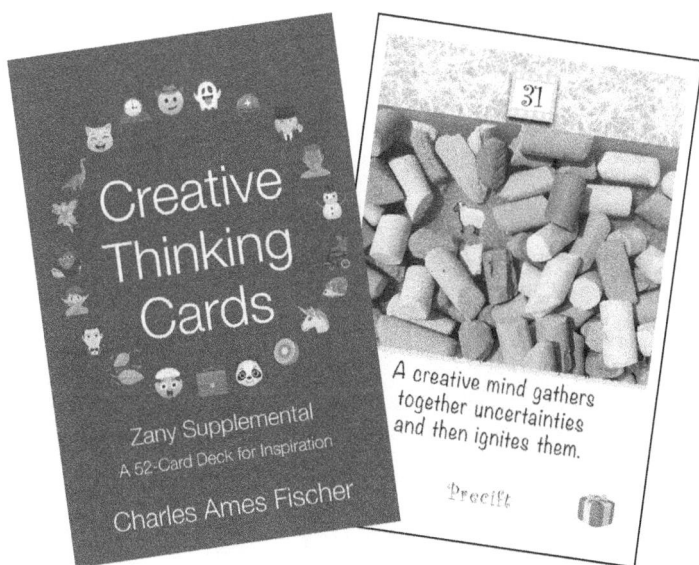

Nauticara Story-World Cards

If pictures are worth a thousand words, then card spreads can generate countless stories. Enter the nautical story-world of Nauticara, where cards are magical and card readings are much more than oracles. Each card in the deck has oracle text for readings, as well as specific story starters that can generate hours of imaginative engagement. Nauticara is an amazing adventure. Discover them on *Deckible.com*.

Filled with numerous story hooks and ideas, these cards can be used for all kinds of creative writing and explorations:

- As writing prompts for creative journaling.
- As original storyboards.
- As an oracle tool for characters in your stories.
- For creating interesting stories-within-stories.

Beyond Infinity

What if numbers came alive? When Matthew discovers a weird computer and a secret door at school, a series of events unfolds where he and his friends solve one mathematical puzzle after another to save 57 and other numbers. *Beyond Infinity* is a fun mathematical MG/YA adventure novel.

Forest School

Forest School is a collection of 48 nature-infused poems that move from the wonders of the forest to the wisdoms of school to the soulful mysteries of transcendence. Here, the forest is both temple and teacher, each poem a tiny doorway. Experience the awe that will awaken the quiet lives inside of you from hibernation.

The Power of the Socratic Classroom
In a Socratic Classroom, teachers shift to the role of facilitator, where they help their students develop the collaborative interpersonal skills, the critical and creative thinking skills, and the speaking and listening skills to face the upcoming challenges of the 21st century. This is the definitive guide to facilitating dialogue in any classroom.

About the Author

Charles Ames Fischer has been a teacher for over 25 years. He's called an audible on a few occasions, stepping out of the classroom to be an education consultant. His flagship book, *The Power of the Socratic Classroom,* won four awards and is hands down one of the most complete guidebooks for facilitating dialogue in K to 12 classrooms. He has also written a novel, *Beyond Infinity,* and created a hat-trick of card decks: *Creative Thinking Cards, Creative Thinking Cards: Zany Edition*, and *Nauticara Story-World Cards*. This is his first collection of poems, soon to be followed by a second, *Forest School.*

He enjoys spending time outdoors, reading middle grades books, watching hockey games and contemplating the meaning of life. Under a full-court press, he would also admit to spending too much time reading fantasy books.

Working With Me

As a consultant and writing coach, Charles offers numerous writing and thinking classes, professional development workshops, Zoom meetings, and more. His primary expertise is Socratic Seminar, with many related areas, such as critical & creative thinking, active listening, close reading, and asking better questions.

Under his guidance, teachers can get the ball rolling to help students achieve more than they ever thought possible.

As an author, Charles is available for school visits, connecting on Zoom, and for book signings. He has a specialty in getting students to hit it out of the park by reading and writing more than they ever thought possible. Learn more at: *CharlesAmesFischer.com.*